The Roaring Twenties and the Great Depression

1920–1940

SADDLEBACK
EDUCATIONAL PUBLISHING

Saddleback's *Graphic American History*

3 7548 00029 3493

SADDLEBACK
EDUCATIONAL PUBLISHING
www.sdlback.com

ISBN-13: 978-1-59905-365-3
ISBN-10: 1-59905-365-9
eBook: 978-1-60291-693-7

Printed in Guangzhou, China
NOR/0413/CA21300730

17 16 15 14 13   4 5 6 7 8 9

At the end of World War I, people were sick of death and destruction and sacrifice. In 1920, Warren G. Harding ran for president on the Republican ticket, conducting a "front-porch" campaign.

What America needs most is a return to normalcy.

People liked the idea. Al Jolson, a popular entertainer, even wrote a song.

Harding you're the man for us, you're the man for us.

For the first time women were able to vote. Many voted for Harding.

He really looks like a nice person.

I know just what you mean.

VOTE HARDING

Election day was Harding's birthday. There was a joint celebration.

You've won a fantastic victory, Mr. President!

It's the biggest popular majority in the nation's history!

But the country failed to return to normalcy.

Industry was geared up for wartime production. Now we have high war taxes and wartime controls, but no orders!

We need a higher protective tariff and help in controlling labor!

But labor, especially the American Federation of Labor, had its own demands.

With no war orders there are not enough jobs. The government must help labor convert to peacetime!

When Harding was elected, the socialist candidate was in the Atlanta penitentiary for antiwar activities.

Eugene V. Debs—941, 827 votes!

Almost a million Socialist votes! I am pleased!

A kindhearted man, Harding made a decision.

Debs has served two years. That is long enough. I will pardon him.

Scandals came to light in the Harding administration. Large amounts of public funds had been misused. There were suicides. Men were convicted of crimes and sent to penitentiaries. Harding did not pardon them!

I can take care of my enemies, but my friends? They're the ones that keep me walking the floor nights!

Perhaps things will seem better after our trip to Alaska.

But already in bad health, during the trip President Harding collapsed and died on August 2, 1923. His return to Washington was as part of a funeral procession.

On August 2, Vice President Calvin Coolidge spent the day raking hay. He slept soundly that night until his father called him.

Calvin?
Mr. President!
President Harding is dead!

The new president's father administered the oath of office in the family sitting room.

Coolidge first came to national attention in 1919, when he was governor of Massachusetts.

Your excellency, the Boston police are threatening to form a labor union.

What does the police commissioner say?

Commissioner Curtis has issued orders banning police membership in labor organizations.

I have no authority over the commissioner, but keep me informed.

The working conditions of the Boston police were scandalously bad.

All through the war we worked for half the salary of war workers.

And now the war is over.

The hours are awful ... Hardly know my children!

And look at this freezing pigpen of a station house.

They had a local organization, the Boston Social Club, where they made plans.

I move we apply to join the American Federation of Labor.

Good! Police in other cities have joined it!

They received a charter and the Central Labor Union of Boston made a statement.

We pledge to the Boston police every atom of support that organized labor can bring to bear!

Then it was the commissioner's turn.

I have found 19 police union leaders guilty of violating my orders! They are suspended from the force.

Do you think the Bolsheviks are behind this?

The policemen voted to leave their posts the next afternoon.

Understand that I do not approve of any strike. But can you blame the police when they get less than a street car conductor?

But they are disobeying my orders!

Bostonians were terrified at the prospect of a police strike.

They say the city will be looted and we will all be assaulted!

Even worse, there's fear that all union men will leave their jobs in a general strike!

It's red agents and anarchists from Russia at the bottom of it—spreading revolution and striking at the very foundations of government!

On Tuesday, 1,117 of Boston's officers walked out. In the early evening, there were only minor disturbances.

Spare tires were stolen from parked cars.

Stop! Stop, thief!

Buzz off!

A trolley car was stoned.

End of the line!

Everybody off!

After midnight, looting and riots began.

Many citizens were robbed.

At dawn, the mayor called out the state guard, resident in Boston, and asked Governor Coolidge for 3,000 additional troops. Before nightfall, guardsmen were patrolling the streets with rifles and fixed bayonets.

In South Boston, they fired on a rioting crowd.

Two men were killed and others wounded.

In Scollay Square, one man died when the cavalry charged a mob.

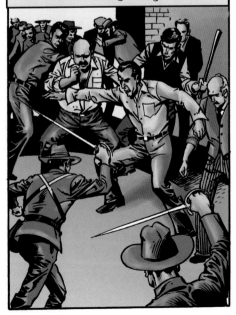

By morning, the situation was under control. Governor Coolidge issued a proclamation essentially approving the mayor's action. But newspapers throughout the country carried stories of the strike, the disorders, and of Coolidge. He had become a great national figure. Elected vice president, he became president upon Harding's death.

To a child of the 1920s, there were many new things—for instance, radio.

Listen, the president.

The business of America is business.

Here in our own living room, we can hear the president speak.

I don't understand what he means.

Sh! Just listen!

The movies were new, too!

KNIGHTS of the KU KLUX KLAN

A famous one showed Southern scenes after the Civil War.

The radio also was reporting similar news.

Yesterday in Georgia, a hooded mob of Ku Klux Klansmen stormed a jail and kidnapped a black man. Later he was beaten, tortured, and burned to death.

How can people be so awful?

I thought the Ku Klux Klan was something back in history!

I am afraid some ignorant, misguided people have revived the Klan in the South and Midwest. They are against anything different from themselves: foreigners, Jews, Catholics, blacks ...

It makes no difference! Just remember this: everyone is entitled to a trial—a fair trial! And no mob has the right to take the law into its own hands!

But was that person a bad man?

One American who fought all his life against the ignorance, intolerance, and prejudice that lead to such injustices was Clarence Darrow, the great lawyer. In 1925, he was approached by members of the NAACP.

Mr. Darrow, did you know that Dr. Ossian Sweet has been charged with murder?

Dr. Sweet, murder? No!

I know Ossian Sweet is a young black man who worked his way through the Howard College medical school, and established a good practice in Detroit! What has happened?

Dr. Sweet and his wife, Gladys, had saved $3,500 to buy a new home. They could find nothing suitable in Detroit's small, cramped African-American community. A real estate agent showed them a house they liked, in a white neighborhood.

Of course, I like it! But...

It is in a white neighborhood.

You'll have no trouble, I'm sure! There are black families living only a block away.

The Sweets spent their savings for the house, and moved in.

Oh, Ossian, I love it! If only people will let us enjoy it.

I have asked for police protection.

If they'll give us a chance, I'm sure we can show people we're no threat.

Our house and yard will be as well kept up as anyone's!

Dr. Sweet's brothers came to help and two of Gladys' friends.

We left the baby with her grandparents, but so far everyone has been pleasant.

What a lovely house, Gladys!

Work done, they sat down to coffee and cake.

What's that?

Something hit the house!

A rock had crashed against the side of the house.

There must be 300 or 400 people out there!

There're two policemen walking up and down.

Pulling down all the shades, making up beds on the floors, the group spent an uneasy night as an occasional rock was thrown. But nothing more serious happened, and the next morning the crowd was gone. Thankful, the Sweets went downtown to shop.

When they came home, there were three friends waiting.

There's talk all over town. They're out to get you, Ossian.

We're here to help. If you want to leave, we'll move your furniture out. It you want to stay, we'll stay with you.

I'm staying. This is my home. I have a right to live in America anywhere I choose, or democracy is a word without meaning!

That night the crowd came back. Insults were shouted, rocks hit the walls. No one inside tried to sleep.

Do you have your gun, Henry? We have a right to defend ourselves and protect Gladys.

It's here.

Suddenly there was a crash.

They're moving forward. I think they're moving in!

Fire high over the crowd, Henry. Let them know we're armed.

Ossian Sweet, too, fired over the heads of the crowd.

There were shots from outside, too— maybe the police.

The mob became individuals, each running to get away.

Someone's hurt!

There's a man dead out here and another injured—shot!

But we fired high over their heads!

You'll have to come with us, all of you!

Don't worry, we'll straighten it out.

That was the story Clarence Darrow heard.

Everyone in the house has been arrested and held. Henry and Ossian Sweet are changed with murder.

What are we waiting for? Let's get to Detroit!

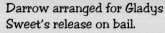

Darrow arranged for Gladys Sweet's release on bail.

It is impossible now to prove whether the deadly shot came from inside the house or from a policeman's gun.

You don't mean the case is hopeless?

Indeed not! We must persuade the jury that a black man has the right to buy a house; the right to live in it; and the right to defend it—just as any other American has!

Darrow concentrated his efforts on the selection of the jury—and its education.

Do you know anything, sir, about the history of the African people in America?

No. I don't think so.

Have you never heard of Frederick Douglass? No?

Have you ever heard of a black man named Banneker? He helped plan the design of the city of Washington, D.C.

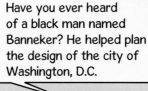

Do you know that the first American to fall in the American Revolution was a black man? Crispus Attucks?

Now let me tell you a little about that great American Frederick Douglass ...

Your honor, I protest! Mr. Darrow is not questioning the jurors. He is trying to instruct them.

I see nothing wrong with what Mr. Darrow is doing. He has as much right to select the jury as you, and the right to do it in his own way.

Turning the routine matter of jury selection into a school for social ideas, Darrow completed his choice.

The case is won or lost now.

Yes, the rest is just window dressing.

Each lawyer presented his case. The jury deliberated. At last it returned to the courtroom.

Have you reached a verdict?

We have, Your Honor.

We find the defendants not guilty!

The National Association for the Advancement of Colored People was an inter-racial organization founded in 1909. Through the NAACP lawyers, such as Clarence Darrow and Arthur Garfield Hays, gave their services to defend the rights of African Americans.

In 1919, U. S. Attorney General Palmer was worried about foreign agitators and communists.

The FBI agent went to W. E. B. Du Bois' office.

This Du Bois over at the NAACP prints strong editorials about the right of blacks. Find out if he is a dangerous radical.

Just what is this organization fighting for?

We are fighting for the enforcement of the Constitution of the United States.

But in the South, the Constitution seemed to mean less and less. Senator Bilbo of Mississippi spoke.

We, the people of the South, must draw the color line tighter and tighter. The white is the custodian of the Gospel of Jesus Christ.

Du Bois had met with other black leaders at Niagara Falls in 1905.

Working peaceably with white people to get the ballot for black people is not working. We are losing ground.

We must turn to the courts and fight for our rights as freeborn Americans.

The Niagara leaders joined with other groups to found the NAACP. Du Bois was offered a new job.

Du Bois, will you take on the job of publicity director and editor of a magazine, the *Crisis*?

I'll accept gladly!

For 25 years, Du Bois edited the *Crisis*. He exposed discrimination. He wrote fiery political editorials, and he had another message.

I want our people to be proud they are black. Black is beautiful!

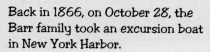

Back in 1866, on October 28, the Barr family took an excursion boat in New York Harbor.

When will we see it?

Any minute now.

Will we see President Cleveland?

Ooooh! Look!

Liberty Enlightening the World, it is called!

This is an historic day. I want you to remember it.

The people of France raised one million francs to give the statue to the people of America. She is holding up the torch of freedom.

President Cleveland spoke at the dedication, accepting the gift for the American People.

We will not forget that Liberty has here made her home.

Most Americans did not see the statue often. But to millions of immigrants, it became their first sight of America, the promise of a new life.

There, little one! See? The Statue of Liberty!

They had come by the millions, from every land, to help build America. Many had gone west to farm.

But now the good land was taken; there were no more homesteads.

They had worked on the railroads.

But now people were traveling by automobile. Nobody was building railroads.

They had been willing to take the worst jobs, the hardest labor.

NO MEN WANTED

But now there were machines, and too many laborers.

Because of the American policy of unrestricted immigration, there had always been a pool of newcomers willing to fill vacant job openings. Labor leaders saw it as a danger.

The companies have restrictive tariffs to protect their goods from cheaper foreign goods, but they can bring in all the cheap labor they want to compete with us and keep our wages low!

At the AFL Convention of 1892, Samuel Gompers reported.

Unrestricted immigration is working a great injury to the people of the country.

The first restrictive act became law in 1921. In his message to Congress of 1923, Coolidge expressed approval.

American institutions were created by people who had a background of self-government. America must be kept American. It is necessary to continue a policy of restricted immigration.

Coolidge got more than he wanted. The final Johnson Immigration Act of 1924 set up a quota system strictly limiting the number of immigrants and sharply favoring those from northern Europe. As it did not apply to immigrants from the New World, those from Canada, Mexico, and the West Indies greatly increased. The Senate also included a provision keeping out all Japanese. Japanese resentment contributed to the rise of militarism in Japan and led toward World War II.

The first automobiles were called horseless carriages, and were made in France.

As president, Theodore Roosevelt took two auto rides, and was stopped for speeding on the second one.

He would not take another until he was out of office, because of the unfavorable publicity.

Frightened horses and timid drivers made automobiles unpopular.

Frequent detours were necessary.

NO HORSELESS CARRIAGES ALLOWED

Cars were expensive and only for the rich. As president of Princeton, Woodrow Wilson warned his students.

Do not indulge in the snobbery of motoring. Nothing has spread socialistic feelings more than this picture of the arrogance of wealth.

A young mechanic in Detroit had a new idea.

Most auto companies make one sample car, and then take orders, only producing custom-made cars already ordered. This makes them too expensive!

I want to make a car that's light but rugged, simple and reliable enough for anybody to run, and cheap enough for every American to buy.

Sounds great, Henry!

Why not make one automobile just like another? All of them can be built just alike, as one pin is like another pin when it comes from a pin factory.

Can you do it?

Mostly on faith and credit, the Ford Motor Company was organized. Soon Henry Ford was producing the car he had described, and American life was changed forever.

There is no other rugged, all-purpose car selling for under $1,500. My price is $825!

NO SM.

In 1916, over 500,000 were sold. In 1923, two million. By 1925, the price was down to $260.

I sure could use one of those new Model-Ts—but that's a lot of cash.

How about so much down and so much a month?

Installment buying, too, was something new. It spread rapidly.

At home, the farmer could jack up a rear wheel and saw wood.

The family could go to town at night.

Anything good at the movies?

The new Clara Bow picture's at the Orpheum!

Well, let's go! Go!

And the next Sunday ...

You're not going to church?

No, dear. You're going to drive us to the country for a nice picnic!

Times were changing. Ideas were changing. But not everybody's and not everywhere.

It's a crime and a shame the way people run around in automobiles on Sunday instead of attending church!

And the modern clothes! And the ideas! Why some people don't even believe in the Bible!

Dayton, Tennessee, was a small, quiet town, until the summer of 1925.

What's going on here, anyway?

Everybody's come to see William Jennings Bryan take to pieces that atheist lawyer, Clarence Darrow!

What in the world can you mean?

Why, Tennessee's got a new law against teaching evolution in the schools—the idea that we're descended from monkeys!

Darwin's *Origin of the Species*, you mean?

It's contrary to the Bible. This young teacher, Scopes, was teaching it in his biology class. 'Course it's in the book he's used for years, but just the same it's against the law now.

Out on the street, the stranger was greeted by banners.

GOD IS LOVE
READ YOUR BIBLE
WE ARE NOT APES
WE ARE MEN

He stopped before a store window.

IS MAN DESCENDED FROM A MONKEY?
IS THIS YOUR GRANDFATHER?

Well, I'll be a monkey's uncle!

Some Protestants believed that everything in the Bible was literally true. They were known as *Fundamentalists.* Bryan spent the declining years of his life fighting to keep school children from being taught modern scientific theories, which conflicted with Fundamentalist beliefs.

Read all about it! Get Mr. Bryan's book, *Hell and the High Schools!*

It's a circus!

Bryan was the prosecutor. The defense lawyers, from the American Civil Liberties Union, included Clarence Darrow, Arthur Garfield Hays, and Dr. Charles F. Potter, a Unitarian minister.

Darrow discussed the case with the others.

Churches and state were separated in America long ago. No one like Bryan has the right to impose his beliefs on American school children.

What about the kids who are Buddhists? Jews? Muslim? Religion should be taught in churches. The schools must be free for young minds to inquire into all beliefs!

The trial was best summed up by Will Rogers, America's beloved humorist.

I like Bill Bryan, but he is making a fool out of himself and out of religion.

Scopes was fined $100, the fine later revoked. The Tennessee law remained on the books. Publicity was the main result of the trial.

Another attempt to legislate people into good behavior was the 18th Amendment to the Constitution.

On January 16, 1920, the 18th Amendment will go into effect prohibiting the manufacture, transportation, and sale of alcoholic beverages.

How wonderful, after all these years! The churches and the Anti-Saloon League have worked so hard!

Well, I think it's a dirty trick! Drinking liquor is as American as apple pie!

But son, the saloons! The lower classes! The laborers spend their money and drink and the poor little children go hungry!

Oh, I know, Mother. It's probably a good thing for the country.

Many motorists drove into the New York State wine country to stock up on champagne and were stranded in a snow storm.

Former President Taft was one of the few people who doubted the success of prohibition.

The business of manufacturing alcohol, liquor, and beer will go out of the hands of law-abiding members of the community, and be transferred to the quasi-criminal class.

But nobody paid attention. On January 16, 10,000 drys attended a mock funeral for John Barleycorn, the make-believe figure who symbolized drink. Billy Sunday, a famous evangelist, conducted the service.

Goodbye, John. You were God's worst enemy. The slums will soon be only a memory. We will turn our prisons into factories! Women will smile and children will laugh again!

In Chicago, only an hour after prohibition started, six masked men entered a railroad yard.

Up with your hands, and into that shed over there!

Leaving the guards bound and gagged, the robbers removed $100,000 worth of medicinal liquor from freight cars.

That's it! Let's go.

Liquor was smuggled into the country from Europe, from Canada, from the Bahamas, Mexico, Cuba. Being both profitable and against the law, smuggling and bootlegging soon became the livelihood of organized crime gangs.

The Coast Guard fought battles with smugglers.

Federal agents raided speakeasies— clubs that sold drinks secretly.

All right, everybody— this is a raid!

Prohibition did not stop anybody who wanted to drink. People called their bootleggers instead of the package stores.

Hello, Charlie? I'd like six bottles of Scotch and three gin for a party tomorrow night. Good! I'll expect it!

It did make drinking and breaking the law acceptable things for the great middle class, for women as well as men. It increased bribery and corruption of law officials, promoted criminals, gangs, slums, warfare, protection rackets, and violence. It did not wipe out slums and poverty. It did not eliminate the problem of alcoholism. And it demonstrated that in a democracy, even the law of the land cannot be enforced without the people behind it.

Twenty-five-year-old Charles A. Lindbergh, an American flying from Roosevelt Field, Long Island, had made the first solo flight across the Atlantic, in 33½ hours. At Le Bourget airdrome he was almost mobbed by the crowd of 25,000.

1927 was also the year when Babe Ruth hit 60 home runs for the New York Yankees.

That September, 150,000 people watched in Chicago as Gene Tunney kept his heavyweight title against ex-champ Jack Dempsey.

It was also big news that millions of people heard the fight by radio.

Another popular sport was getting something for nothing, or playing the stock market.

... claims that Tunney got a long count in the 7th round, and will contest the decision.

I think Dempsey got robbed, don't you, Dad?

I guess we'll have to leave it to the officials.

It's lovely. But I just can't afford it.

But my dear! Buy a few shares of stock on margin and wait a few days for it to go up!

That night she asked her husband about the stock market.

Yes, a lot of people are making money on the stock market. Usually prices go up for awhile, and then down again. But lately, they've kept going up.

Does it take a lot of money to buy stock?

Well, people are buying "on margin." Say you put up $100, and the broker lends you $300 and buys you $400 worth of stock. If it doubles in price, he sells it for $800, keeps his $300, and you've made $500!

It sounds like magic!

Calling it speculation sounds more professional!

So long as stocks keep going up, people keep buying them—and as long as people keep buying them, they keep going up! What's the catch?

In the past, what goes up has always come down again. If you don't pick the right time to sell, both you and the stockbroker have lost your money. But now some people think it can go up forever, and everybody can be rich.

Herbert Hoover, a Republican, was elected president to succeed Coolidge in 1928. He made a prediction.

We shall soon with the help of God be in sight of the day when poverty will be banished from this nation.

But in October 1929, the stock market collapsed with a crash.

No!

It was one of the worst days in history. Millions went bankrupt.

The market collapse set off a chain reaction in the economy. Stores cancelled orders.

People are not buying! I'll cancel orders at the factory. And we don't need all these salespeople.

At the factories, canceled orders meant too much stock on hand.

Sorry, men, this section's being shut down. We'll call you if things pick up again.

When there were no more paychecks, people lost the things they had been buying on the installment plan.

The furniture went ...	Then the car ...	Then even the house ...

We'll replace it as soon as I have a job.

I don't know how we'll get along without a car!

Maybe walking will be good for us.

Big corporations that had speculated in the stock market went into bankruptcy and closed.

Banks that had made big loans to brokers could not collect them, and were forced to close.

It's locked! Closed up!

It can't be! All my savings are there.

In 1930, breadlines appeared in American cities.

As unemployment and hunger increased throughout the country, liberal congressmen like Senator Cutting talked to Hoover.

Mr. President, the federal government must do something to help our people!

Direct federal aid is against all my principles! If a bill is passed, I will veto it.

Shanty towns grew up near many cities. People called them "Hoovervilles."

People without homes drove from place to place. There might be a job somewhere else, but there never was.

By 1932, 5,000 banks had failed and more than 15 million people were out of work. In Portland, Oregon, World War I veterans had an idea.

I was thinking about that bill Congress passed after the war, promising to pay us a bonus in 1945.

I'll be starved to death before 1945.

We sure could use the money now.

So why don't we march to Washington and petition Congress for it?

It would beat hanging around here starving to death.

Electing Walter Waters their leader, the unemployed veterans started for Washington.

Strict discipline, now! No panhandling, no drinking, no radicalism!

Easy to tell he was a sergeant!

Veterans all over the country heard of the idea and joined in. From every state, they headed for Washington, walking, riding freight cars, or driving in old jalopies.

Brought your family too, did you?

Sure, lost our home, anyway.

About 15,000 reached Washington, and built a shack-village on Anacostia Flats.

Hey, Dad! I found a swell piece of cardboard.

Pelham D. Glassford was the head of Washington's Metropolitan Police Force. He had served in World War I himself, the youngest general in France.

These are good guys. Don't, hassle them! I want to find them some food.

Glassford understood the veterans, and sympathized with them. He requisitioned an army field kitchen to feed them.

Boy, this is real food.

The House of Representatives passed a bill to pay the veterans their bonus. On June 17, the bill came up in the Senate. To the veterans gathered outside, Waters brought the news.

Comrades, I have bad news. The Senate defeated the bill.

Comrades, show them that we are patriotic Americans. Let's sing "America."

The men sang, then quietly went back to their shacks.

Some of those boys soldiered for me. They're my boys.

They're no mob—they're just unlucky Americans!

President Hoover refused to receive the veterans' representatives, to visit them, to acknowledge their existence. By July, most had returned home. But 2,000 remained.

Where've I got to go to? This is as good a home as I've had for two years.

I'm trying to set up some camps in the country near here. You could farm, maybe even set up light manufacturing.

On July 28, Secretary of War Hurley sent for Army Chief of Staff Douglas MacArthur.

There veterans are a mob, a threat to the American government! Clear them out.

Yes, sir! I have released in my day more than one community which had been held in the grip of a foreign enemy.

44

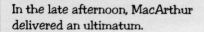

In the late afternoon, MacArthur delivered an ultimatum.

You people have exactly one hour to clear out!

But sir, these are our homes.

As evening fell, four troops of cavalry, six tanks, and a column of infantry moved in.

Please sir, my pet rabbit's in there.

Get away from here, you ...

All over the country people were shocked when they saw the scenes on movie newsreel and heard radio comment.

What a pitiful spectacle is that of the great American government chasing unarmed men, women, and children with army tanks and bayonets.

What's happening to the country! It can't go on this way!

Some people say communism's the way out.

Or fascism.

There's a presidential election this year. It's our chance to find a leader who can make democracy work again.

The Republicans renominated Herbert Hoover. He warned the country against electing a Democrat.

Any change of policy will bring disaster to every fireside in America!

Don't he know we've already got disaster?

Blacks are the last hired, the first fired. We've suffered longer than anybody in this depression.

We've been Republicans. Now it's time we vote for bread and butter, instead of the memory of Abe Lincoln.

The Democrats nominated Franklin D. Roosevelt. He traveled across the country campaigning.

I pledge you, I pledge myself, to a new deal for the American people.

Roosevelt was elected by a big majority. On inauguration day, March 7, 1933, he spoke to a desperate nation.

This nation will endure ... will revive and prosper. Let me assert my firm belief that the only thing we have to fear is fear itself. The nation asks for action, and action now.

Will Rogers expressed the peoples' feelings.

America hasn't been as happy in three years ... No money, no work, no nothing, but they know they got a man in there.

Why is the new president lame?

His legs were crippled by polio. He has fought for years to get back on his feet again.

It seems to give him an understanding of the hardships other people have to face.

The cabinet was sworn in that same day, and Roosevelt met with them.

I am calling Congress into special session at once. We must take immediate relief measures; then longer-term recovery measures.

The first measure was the Emergency Banking Act.

Perhaps it is necessary to nationalize the banks.

I don't want to replace the banking system; I want to save it.

The president declared a bank holiday. Then the banks reopened on a sounder basis. Later, an insurance system was set up to protect depositors against loss if a bank failed.

I want to establish a conservation corps, to help preserve the countryside at the same time it gives employment to our young men.

Perhaps the army could run the camps.

And labor could administer them.

By July, 300,000 boys were working in 1,300 camps over the country earning wages and eating regularly for the first time in their lives. They came from families on relief, and a part of their earnings went to their families.

They planted trees where the soil was blowing away.

They built irrigation dams.

They improved the national parks.

The Federal Emergency Relief Act provided $500 million for direct relief to states, cities, towns, counties. Harry Hopkins was put in charge.

I want you as my relief administrator, Harry.

The people want jobs, not handouts. As far as possible, I will make it a work-relief program.

Money went at once to feed the starving. And by November, Hopkins had four million people at work under the Civil Works Administration.

They worked on roads, built sewers, playgrounds, and parks.

The CWA also employed teachers for adult education courses.

Important to all of the president's accomplishments was his wife, Eleanor.

I want to tell you about the project I visited today.

Eleanor is my eyes and ears and sometimes my conscience!

In May, a new bonus army of veterans gathered in Washington—still thin, hungry, shabby. But there was a difference.

The leaders were asked to an immediate meeting with the president. Later, they had a visitor.

You mean the president's giving us an army camp to live in?

Yes, and three meals a day.

Is there any thing you need? Is the food good? Has an army doctor seen all your sick people?

Hoover sent the army. Roosevelt sent his wife!

One of Eleanor Roosevelt's friends was Mary McLeod Bethune, an African-American educator.

Sixty-nine percent of the blacks in southern cities need relief—and they get only what's leftover from the needy whites.

In the federal programs, no discrimination will be allowed. And a percentage of the administrators must be blacks.

The thing that's hardest to bear is seeing the hopelessness of our young people. Their job chances are poor, but their chances of an education have almost disappeared.

They must be helped! Educating our people is vital!

The National Youth Administration was set up to help young people continue their educations, and Mary McLeod Bethune became director of minority affairs.

The NYA spent millions of dollars helping a critical age group, black and white.

The farmers had been the forgotten man for many years. Roosevelt talked to the secretary of agriculture, Wallace.

Since World War I, prices have been so low that the farmers have had to raise more and more to make ends meet, and the surplus has led to still lower prices!

Suppose we paid the farmer not to plant so many crops—to give the demand a chace to catch up with the supply?

The Agricultural Adjustment Act did far more than this, but this was the principle that caused the most criticism.

Roosevelt cared about people—and the people wrote to tell him their troubles.

Is this all?

All? There are several truckloads still to come.

Roosevelt met with labor leaders, George Meany of the AFL, and John L. Lewis of the United Mine Workers.

It seems obvious to me that workers should be protected in their right to join unions, and to bargain collectively.

The National Labor Relations Act guaranteed these rights.

The Tennessee, 625 miles long, is one of the great North American rivers. Draining an area having the second highest rainfall in the country, it became a destructive torrent every spring.

Senator George Norris of Nebraska, a liberal Republican, for many years had had plans for the Tennessee Valley.

It is a sad, poverty-stricken area of eroded farmland, but it could be redeemed.

Two of my bills for a dam and flood control project passed Congress, but were vetoed by Presidents Coolidge and Hoover.

I can picture dams, cheap electric power, reforestation, farmland reclaimed, new local industries ... draft another bill!

The bill setting up a Tennessee Valley Authority—the TVA—was signed by Roosevelt on May 18, 1933.

This act will reclaim an area almost as large as England!

This is the most wonderful and far-reaching humanitarian document that has ever come from the White House.

The TVA built flood-control dams ...

Great locks for commercial navigation ...

Plants for generating electricity ...

With few compulsory powers, TVA works through local authorities, with voluntary cooperation by individuals. 54,000 farms, with more than 6.6 million acres, have taken part in its improvement program.

★ ★ ★ ★ ★ ★ ★

More than 200 private companies manufacture and market products developed by TVA. Since World War II, it has been the model for similar projects in many parts of the world.

In 1934, the Roosevelts drove through cheering but poverty-stricken crowds to visit the half-completed Norris Dam.

Six years later, the TVA projects had had time to show results.

The old people of America had been harder hit than any other group except the African Americans. Roosevelt did not want that to continue.

It would be hard to find a more prosperous area!

I want to set up a system of old-age insurance, to which both employees and employers will contribute. At the age of 65, workers will receive a monthly retirement income.

It should also include disability insurance. And unemployment insurance. And aid to dependent mothers and children.

In the election of 1936, the Republicans nominated Governor Alfred Landon of Kansas, the sunflower state. They campaigned with sunflower ties and hats.

The Social Security Act of 1935 was a landmark in establishing our government's social responsibility to citizens.

They also attacked the New Deal.

The CWA, OCC, TVA, WPA! Alphabet soup! These are gigantic boondoggles.

For four years you have had an administration which instead of twirling its thumbs has rolled up its sleeves ... We will continue to seek improved working conditions ... to end monopoly in business ... we have only just begun to fight.

Roosevelt, his family, and friends, awaited the election returns at his Hyde Park home.

Congratulations, Mr. President! You have won by the biggest landslide in history.

The people have given unmistakable approval of your policies.

The New Deal relieved the distress of unemployment. It did much for the physical rehabilitation of the country and to stop the waste of natural resources. It developed the idea that the federal government is responsible for the people's welfare.

★★★★★★

It established economic and social planning by the federal government. Most important of all, it gave the American people new faith in their democratic system.